Indian Nations

THE MAKAH

by
Jeanne Oyawin Eder

General Editors
Herman J. Viola and Felix C. Lowe

A Rivilo Book

RSVP
RAINTREE
STECK-VAUGHN
PUBLISHERS
A Steck-Vaughn Company

Austin, Texas
www.steck-vaughn.com

Published by Raintree Steck-Vaughn Publishers, an imprint of Steck-Vaughn Company.

Developed for Steck-Vaughn Company
by Rivilo Books
Editor: David Jeffery
Photo Research: Paula Dailey
Design: Barbara Lisenby
Electronic Preparation: Curry Printing

Raintree Steck-Vaughn Publishers Staff
Publishing Director: Walter Kossmann
Editor: Kathy DeVico
Design Project Manager: Lyda Guz

Photo Credits: Richard A. Cooke III/National Geographic Society (NGS) Image Collection: cover; Lisa Ranallo Horsecapture: illustration: pp. 4, 6, 7, 8; Edward S. Curtis/NGS Image Collection: p. 9; Richard A. Cooke III: pp. 10, 17, 22 top, 22 bottom, 24 top, 25 top, 27 top, 28, 29, 34, 37 top; Herman Viola: pp. 12, 18, 19 top, 20 bottom; Archive Photos: p. 13; Glenbow-Alberta Institute, Calgary: p. 14; Museum of History and Industry, Seattle, Washington: p. 16; Makah Cultural and Research Center: pp 31, 32, 36, 40; Richard Schlecht/NGS Image Collection: pp. 20 left, 25 bottom, 26; Samuel Morse/Washington State Historical Society (WSHS), Tacoma: p. 21; Bates Littlehales/NGS Image Collection: p. 22 center; Edward A. Curtis/WSHS: p. 24 bottom; WSHS: p. 27 bottom, 30; Theresa Parker: p. 37, 39 top; AP/Wide World Photo: p. 38; Thad Samuels Abell II/NGS Image Collection: p. 39 bottom. The following images were photographed courtesy of the Makah cultural and Research Center: pp. 12 bottom, 19 bottom, 22 top, 22 bottom, 25 top, 27 top, 28 bottom, 34, 36, 40.

We wish to thank Janine Bowechop, Keely Parker and Ray Colby.

Library of Congress Cataloging-in-Publication Data
Eder, Jeanne M. Oyawin.
    The Makah/by Jeanne Oyawin Eder.
        p. cm — (Indian nations)
    Includes bibliographical references and index.
    Summary: Introduces the history, culture, religion, family life, and tribal government of the Makah people.
        ISBN 0-8172-5459-5
        1. Makah Indians — Juvenile literature.   [1. Makah Indians.
    2. Indians of North America — Washington (State)]   I. Title.
    II. Series: Indian nations (Austin, Tex.)
    E99.M19E38   2000
    979.7'004979 — dc21   99-23350
                                                     CIP
            2469496

Printed and bound in the United States of America.
1 2 3 4 5 6 7 8 9 0 LB 03 02 01 00 99

Contents

Makah Folktale

Hundreds of years ago in Native American Indian culture, there were no written languages. Tribal history was passed to each generation by elders telling stories to children. Most tribes had their own story of the creation of the Earth and explanations for common natural events that often involved the actions of animals. Here is one **Makah** (Ma-KAW) story.

Raven Steals the Daylight

Long ago, there was a time when only darkness surrounded the Earth. This time was before water covered the Earth and before there were trees and animals. This was before birds flew and fish swam in the seas. In this darkness lived an old man and his daughter. They lived in a house along a river.

Raven also lived at this time, because Raven has always been on Earth. But Raven was not happy because he stumbled around in darkness and kept bumping into things. As he wandered, he came near the house of the old man. He heard chanting coming from inside the house. When he put his ear against the wall he heard these words: "I have a box and inside the box is another box and inside that box is another box and inside are many more boxes, and inside the tiniest box is all the daylight in the universe. And all of it is mine, and I will never give it to anyone. I will not give it to my daughter, because she may be ugly, and we do not need to know that."

Raven decided to steal the box. He went to the river to wait for the old man and his daughter to come for water. He began

◄ *Eagle chases Raven, who stole daylight from an old man.*

5

to imagine the young daughter. Perhaps she was beautiful, but perhaps she was as ugly as a sea slug.

When Raven heard the footsteps of the young daughter, he changed himself into a hemlock (pine) needle. He dropped into the river and floated down to where the young daughter was dipping her basket into the water. Raven made more magic. He made the young daughter thirsty, and she took a drink from her basket of water. She swallowed the hemlock needle. Raven slid down her throat and into her belly. Raven then changed himself into a tiny human being and went to sleep. As he slept, he began to grow.

The young daughter had no idea what was happening to her. She did not tell her father, and because it was dark, her father could not see his daughter getting bigger. One day Raven was born as a human boy child, but he had a long beaked nose, a few feathers, and the shining eyes of a raven.

At times Raven cried like a spoiled baby. At other times he talked softly like wind blowing through hemlock boughs. The old man loved this new member of the household and spent hours with Raven, making him toys and playing games with him. When Raven had explored all of the house, he became certain that daylight must be hidden in the big box he had found in a corner of the house. One day Raven lifted the lid of the box, and all he could feel was another box. The old man heard Raven disturb the box and punished him. But Raven still wanted to get the boxes from the old man. So on one day Raven would cry for the box like a spoiled child, and on another day he used his soft voice to plead for the box. As all grandfathers finally do, the old man gave in and let Raven have the first box. As all young grandchildren do, Raven pleaded for another box.

It took many days, but finally Raven had nearly all the boxes. When only a few were left, a strange light and shadows began to appear in the house. Raven asked to open the last box and hold the daylight inside for just a moment. Again, his grandfather gave in, and the old man lifted the ball of daylight from the final box and gave it to his grandson, Raven.

The old man had only a glimpse of his grandson, because Raven changed from his human form to his old self—with a large beak and huge black wings. Raven caught the ball of light in his beak and, with one flap of his wings, flew into the air.

At once the world was changed. The silhouettes of mountains stood against the sky, and the valleys were visible. Rivers sparkled, and everywhere life began to appear.

From far away Eagle caught sight of Raven and began to chase him. Raven swerved to escape Eagle and dropped part of the daylight. It fell to the ground and broke into one large piece and many smaller ones. Those pieces bounced back into the sky and became the moon and the stars.

Eagle flew after Raven again and chased him to the rim of the world. Raven was so tired that he let go of his last piece of daylight. It floated on the clouds and finally started to rise over the mountains in the east.

The first rays of the sun lit up the house of the old man, where he sat weeping for having been tricked by his grandson. But as light entered the house, the old man looked at his daughter for the first time and saw that she was beautiful, and he wept for joy.

Settlement and Geography

Indians of the Makah Nation live on the Northwest Pacific Coast of the United States. Their home is in the very northwest corner of the Olympic Peninsula in the state of Washington. The Makah are one of many tribes that belong to the Northwest Coast Culture. Other tribes in this region are the Haida, Kwakiutl, Nootka, and Tlingit. In the past, many of these tribes spoke distinct languages, but they shared similar lifestyles. They lived in large wooden houses and erected large wooden posts, known as totem poles, which featured carvings of animals and mythical creatures. The tribes in this region also all lived primarily from the bounty of the sea.

To sustain their villages, Makah hunters used harpoons buoyed by sealskin floats to claim gray whales from the Pacific Ocean.

The Makah live on the Pacific Coast in what is now Washington State.

The many tribes of this culture occupy a long narrow belt of land along the coast of the Pacific Ocean. It stretches more than 1,500 miles (2,414 km) from southeastern Alaska to the redwood forests of northwestern California. The climate there is mild and pleasant, though rain falls frequently throughout the year. The summers are mostly cool, and the winters are mild and wet.

The Makah and other Northwest Coast peoples did not have to work extremely hard to get enough to eat. The Pacific Ocean and the region's many rivers supplied plenty of fish, especially salmon and halibut. Other marine life, and whales in particular, were very important to the Makah, both as food and in their culture.

The Makah and their neighbors on the Northwest Coast became expert woodworkers, because the forests provided giant red cedar and other large trees that are easy to split and to carve. The Makah built large wooden canoes, tall totem poles, and huge houses. These wooden houses often had a single large room that was capable of holding a hundred or more people. Their houses were the largest of any built in native North America.

Scientific evidence shows that Makah people have lived in their current location for more than 4,000 years. The Makah, however, believe they have lived there since the beginning of time, or "since the first daylight."

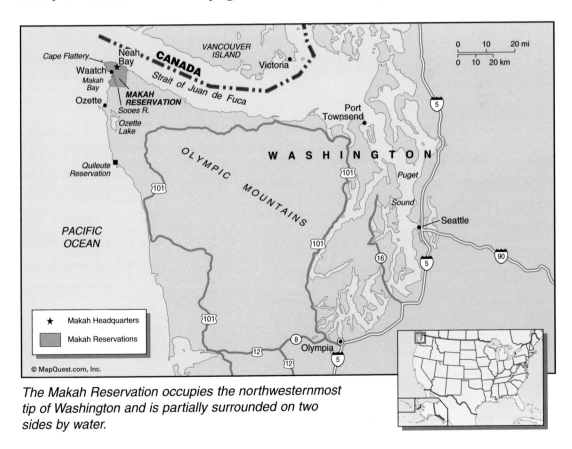

The Makah Reservation occupies the northwesternmost tip of Washington and is partially surrounded on two sides by water.

Ancient Makah petroglyphs found just south of Ozette village.

The Makah originally lived in five permanent villages called Bahaada, Deah (now known as Neah Bay), Waatch, Sooes, and Ozette. These villages were located on the tip of the Olympic Peninsula. The land was bordered by the Pacific Ocean to the west and included many forested mountains and rocky hills to the east.

As with other Indian groups, the Makah spoke their own language. It was slightly different from that of any other Indian tribe and much different from English. In their own language they called themselves **Kwih-ditch-chuh-ahtx** (Kwee-DICH-cha-aht), which in English means "People who live by the rocks and seagulls." They have also been called "People of the Cape" because of their location along what is now known as Cape Flattery. They were given the name Makah by neighboring tribes. In English, the word Makah means "generous with food."

The Makah are closely related to the Nootka, who live north of them on Vancouver Island, in Canada. The Nootka's language is essentially the same, and their lifestyle is very similar. At one time the two tribes may have been a united people.

Makah villages were built on the tip of the Olympic Peninsula.

Key Historical Events

The first known contact between the Northwest Coast Indians and Europeans came in 1774. Juan Pérez Hernandez, a Spanish explorer who was sailing up the coast from California, met Makah and other tribal peoples who paddled out to his ship in their large wooden canoes. Hernandez claimed the entire Pacific Coast as part of Spain's domain in North America, although none of his men actually set foot on land.

More significant was the contact made in 1778 with the famous English explorer James Cook. Cook was sailing through the Bering Strait in search of a northwest passage to China. He and his sailors visited the Nootka and traded knives, axes, and nails with them for sea otter furs.

James Cook, the English explorer, made contact with the Makah in 1778.

John Webber, an artist traveling with Cook, drew the first pictures known in Europe of the Northwest Coast peoples. When Webber asked permission to draw an interior view of a chief's house, he found that the Indians were tough bargainers. The agreed price was several shiny metal buttons from his fancy uniform coat. When Webber started drawing, however, members of the chief's family covered some of the most interesting wooden carvings in the room with blankets and demanded more buttons if he wanted to include them in his picture. Webber was able to finish his drawing but at the cost of most of his uniform buttons. Although he could hardly hold

John Webber made this drawing of the Makah in the the late 1700s.

his pants up when he left the house, Webber possessed one of the most important drawings ever made of the Northwest Coast Indians before their rich culture was forever changed by contact with Europeans.

James Cook failed to find the passage to China, and he was later killed by natives in Hawaii. But his reports about sea otters and other furbearing animals on the Northwest Coast caused a sensation in Europe. Known as "soft gold," these furs brought fabulous prices when sold in China.

After both Cook's journals and Webber's drawings were published in 1784, trading expeditions to the Northwest Coast often came to the area. Europeans knew that they could trade items such as copper and iron to the Indians for furs—sea otter furs in particular. Then the Europeans would trade the furs in China for a large profit. Because the Makah often attacked the traders, they gained a reputation for being fierce and hostile. But the traders kept coming, because they made so much money from the furs.

Besides items useful to the Makah and other Indians, the traders brought with them diseases such as **smallpox**, measles, influenza, and **tuberculosis**, to which the Makah had never been exposed. The Indians' immune systems could not combat the diseases, so many died, including whole villages.

Soon Spanish officers and missionaries, who were devout Roman Catholics, began trying to convert Northwest Coast Indians. The Catholics even traded copper for young Indian slaves in order to Christianize them. As part of these attempts at conversion, the Makah and other Indians were told that their own traditional religion was evil. Despite the Spaniards' efforts, however, the Northwest Coast peoples resisted and drove the Europeans from their lands.

When Americans arrived, they came to stay and brought their own laws with them. In the 1850s, the U.S. government began to take over lands that the Indians had always considered to be their home. Indians were made to live on **reservations**, and the government wanted to control every aspect of their daily lives. American agents told Indians how to dress, forced them to speak English, and replaced traditional learning with government schools. They also tried to suppress Indian use of traditional ceremonies and culture. The entire process was called **assimilation**. Its goal was to extinguish Indian culture and integrate the Makah into mainstream American society.

The U.S. government tried to make the Makah into farmers, but the weather on the Olympic Peninsula was too rainy and the soil too sandy for their crops to succeed. The 1855

Treaty of Neah Bay between the Makah and the U.S. government set standards for Makah community life and allowed them to continue their fishing, including the right to hunt whales. Despite the treaty's promises, whaling was banned in the late 1800s because the population of whales had dropped, due mostly to commercial whaling by non-Indians. As whaling declined, the Makah's pursuit of seals for food and fur trading increased. Many other Makah fishermen were hired or kidnapped by white schooner owners to aid in commercial fishing.

In 1885, for the first time, a Makah man spent the money he had earned on a white-run fishing schooner to buy his own boat. He thus became an employer rather than an employee and could make his own profits with his own property. By the early 1890s, Makah people owned ten such fishing schooners. They profited immensely from the commercial fishing, some making nearly $5,000 per year, a small fortune at that time. Now the tables were turned, as many white people from nearby Port Townsend were hired by Makah boat owners to work during the sealing season.

Sturdy traditional canoes of western red cedar, like these at Neah Bay, served for transportation and hunting.

Despite the Makah's financial prosperity, the U.S. government became concerned that the policy of assimilation was failing. The Makah continued to practice their traditional customs, including **potlatches**. The word potlatch means "giving." The gift-giving ceremony is at the core of Northwest Coast social life (see page 28), but most outsiders misunderstood it. They viewed it as wasteful. In the 1920s, sheriff's deputies armed with shotguns tried to stop the Makah from practicing the potlatch ceremony on a nearby island, but the attempt failed.

In December 1897, the U.S. government banned the hunting of seals by all U.S. citizens except native hunters using traditional methods. The same government that had earlier demanded that the Makah assimilate, or change to the

Potlatch ceremonies still feature dances to celebrate giving gifts to others.

modern methods, was now outlawing those new methods and insisting that the Makah return to their traditional ways. The Makah simply adapted and increased their fishing for halibut. The halibut industry supported the Makah until the 1930s, when non-Indian competition made it much less profitable. Again the Makah adapted. They replaced halibut fishing with more salmon fishing, and it became their primary occupation until the 1970s.

One of the most significant historical events of the Northwest coast occurred in 1970, when parts of the ancient Makah village of Ozette were uncovered by erosion. Hundreds of years earlier, Ozette had been covered by a mudslide. The earth that covered Ozette had remained damp all that time, so it had preserved eight **long houses** and their contents remarkably well. The contents of the site were studied by archaeologists, and the

A big Pacific Ocean storm in 1970 exposed remains of the ancient Makah village of Ozette (below), revealing artifacts and details of long houses (left) that Makah people had lived in for centuries.

artifacts were placed in the care of the Makah people. In 1979 these historical items were placed in the Makah Cultural and Research Center. This center houses exhibits and artifacts from the Ozette discovery. It also has full-scale replicas of a long house, a whaling canoe, and other traditional and modern craft exhibits. The center is used as a resource to help the Makah retain their cultural heritage and pride and to educate others.

The Makah Cultural and Research Center (above) was built to house artifacts from Ozette and other items such as these replicas of whaling canoes (left).

Way of Life

Like most Indian peoples, the Makah utilized fish, animals, and plants for food and to make their lives easier. Their diet consisted of fish such as halibut and salmon, and shellfish, such as clams and mussels. The Makah hunted whales as another main food source from the sea. They fashioned cedar bark, seaweed, and **kelp** to make ropes and fishing lines. Makah men split huge cedar logs to build their houses and make their canoes. They hunted game like elk and deer in the inland forests. Women and children harvested abundant amounts of berries such as salmonberry, blackberry, salal, thimbleberry, and huckleberry. Much of the berry harvest was dried so that the people could eat it later.

Cedar planks were split from living trees (above) using wooden wedges (right) and stone mauls.

Fish were hung to dry from poles in front of long houses where several families lived together.

The Makah lived in large, permanent dwellings called long houses, or great houses. The average size of a long house was about 60 feet (18 m) long, 30 feet (10 m) wide, and 15 feet (5 m) tall. Walls were made of cedar planks attached to poles with ropes made from vines and other natural sources, such as shredded bark and leather strips. Many of these long houses made up a village. Each house was occupied by several small families related to each other through their fathers. This meant that brothers and their families (20 to 30 people) tended to live together in the same house with their father. The father was usually considered a house chief as head of the family lineage.

Clothing and Crafts

Makah clothing was fairly simple due to the comfortable climate of the Pacific coast. Men wore capes made of cedar bark or sea otter skins. Women often wore capes also, as well as skirts made of shredded cedar bark. Both Makah men and women were known for their woven cedar hats.

Makah artisans made many different items for hunting and for their houses. They made all their cooking utensils from wood or bone and used cedar wood to make special boxes to use for storage and for cooking.

Makah artisans used local materials to craft items that were both practical and beautiful. Cedar bark was woven into whaler's hats (above) and baskets (below). Wood, bone, and possibly walrus ivory were used to make finely carved combs (right).

Cedar bark was used to make baskets, ropes, and woven hats. Cedar trees were also used to make totem poles, ceremonial masks, dishes, and utensils. Blankets and rugs were loomed from the fur of dogs, mountain goats, and other animals. Clubs and tools were carved from native stone.

Medicine

The Makah used native plants for medicine. They had natural remedies for everything from tuberculosis to a toothache. The following are a few plants used for treatments:

Licorice fern	roasted, peeled, then chewed and the juice swallowed for coughs
Deer fern and Maidenhair fern	leaves chewed to ease stomach trouble
Hemlock bark	chewed and applied to a wound to stop bleeding
Salmonberry bark	pounded and put on an aching tooth or festering wound to relieve pain

Whaling and the Spiritual Life

Makah legend speaks often of the thunderbird, a huge, powerful bird with sharp talons that was a sacred leader to them. It is said that at one time the Makah ate only fish, but then the

ocean became so rough that they could no longer fish. The thunderbird swooped down from the sky and caught a whale in its talons and brought it to the shore. When morning came, the Makah found a whale on the beach. Since that day they

In legend, the thunderbird (left) first brought the whale to the Makah, and, traditionally, whales were butchered on the beach (below).

Harpoon tips were for whale hunting, large hooks for halibut, small ones for bass.

have hunted and honored the whale and made it a primary source of food. The rights and rituals of whale hunting were passed down by families from generation to generation.

The Makah hunted gray whales, sperm whales, right whales, and humpbacks. An adult gray whale can measure up to 40 feet (12 m) long and weigh nearly 20 tons. The Makah used canoes made of hollowed out cedar trees, measuring nearly 30 feet (9 m) long and 6 feet (2 m) wide. A crew of eight was required to row such a canoe. The 16-foot (5-m) long harpoons were made of yew wood with a rope attached. The harpoon's point was made of a sharpened giant mussel shell with a barb of elk bone.

A whale hunter and his family continually prepared themselves physically and mentally for a hunt. In the months leading up to the hunt, many more intense preparations were made by the whale hunter and his crew. The crew members prayed and fasted, asking the whale to give up its life. The crew purified their bodies and spirits as they bathed in cold streams and lakes all through the winter,

Before the hunt, whalers swim in secret pools. While her husband is at sea, a harpooner's wife lies still to keep the whale calm.

To keep a newly killed whale from sinking, sealskin floats are lashed on, and the animal's mouth is sewn shut.

often imitating the movements of a whale. To toughen their skin, they rubbed their bodies with hemlock twigs and nettles.

When the time came, the hunters paddled several miles out into the ocean. When they spotted a whale, they paddled near it and watched it dive and resurface. Everyone in the canoe silently prayed for good luck. They had to be careful, because one slap of the whale's huge tail could break their canoe. As the whale surfaced, a hunter stood up in the **bow**. He then thrust the harpoon into the whale's side, behind the flipper and toward the whale's heart. The whale was struck as near the heart as possible with several more harpoons. Each harpoon carried floats made of sealskin filled with air and tied to the harpoon rope. The floats prevented the whale from diving. Often, however, the

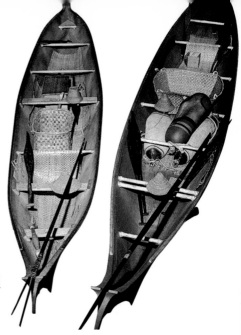

Floats, hats, oars, and harpoons are loaded in canoes before the hunt.

whale towed a canoe miles out into the ocean. Before it tired and died, one of the crew swam out to the whale and tied its mouth shut so that water could not enter and make the whale sink. The whale was then towed back to the village.

The whole village celebrated a successful hunt with songs and dances honoring the crew. The whale's meat was then distributed following a specific system according to the social order. Different families would get different parts of the animal. The Makah used every part of the whale and wasted nothing. A whaling family had the highest status and would get the choicest parts, while a family of a craftsman would get an adequate supply of meat and oil, although from a different part of the whale. Three or four whales would feed the entire village for a year.

Spiritual ceremonies such as those performed in preparation for the whale hunt were of the utmost importance. The Makah believed that all things had a living spirit and often prayed for its help. They prayed with songs and dances that had been passed down for many generations.

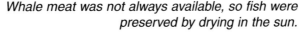

Whale meat was not always available, so fish were preserved by drying in the sun.

Potlatches

A social ceremony widely used by many Northwest Coast Indians was the potlatch, which comes from a Chinook word for giving. A potlatch was a way of gaining honor and celebrating an important event like a birth or death, a coming of age, or recognizing the right of the host to perform an important duty. Ceremonies included special songs, dances, stories, and regalia, as well as a lavish feast. People traveled from other tribes to be included in the celebration. Gifts were given by the host to the guests, and included ceremonial masks, hats, blankets, jewelry, and intricately carved statues. People who received gifts were often then obligated to return the favor by hosting their own potlatch and giving gifts in return.

Elaborate costumes, such as this bird man, were worn at potlatches.

The potlatch ceremony was banned at the turn of the century and for many years, partly because white missionaries were appalled to see such free distribution of personal belongings, which they considered wasteful. But the ban was also an effort by the government to take away native rights and destroy traditional arts, songs, dances, languages, and culture. Some of the Makah people

A 500-year-old carved figure might have been given at an ancient potlatch.

were determined not to lose all of their cultural heritage. They continued to practice the traditional ceremonies for many years in secret. As these people remained faithful to the old ways, many of the ceremonies were kept alive. In the mid-20th century, the U.S. government gave up on the assimilation policy. The Makah and many other Indian tribes were then allowed again to practice publicly their traditional ceremonies, including the potlatch.

Gifts, such as this fine blanket, are still given at modern potlatches.

Family Life

Makah villages consisted of several houses made of long cedar planks. The head of an entire household of several families was called the **headman**. The headman was responsible for his household and all its members. He attended council meetings with other headmen to help make decisions to benefit the village. Within a household, families maintained their own social structure. Rank was determined mainly by age, with the oldest boys having the highest status.

The main role of men was to fish, hunt, and protect their village and families. Many men were also excellent craftsmen. They made the long houses, canoes, and tools, as well as detailed carvings from wood and bones. The most honored of men among the Makah were the whale hunters, seal hunters, and fishermen.

A carved canoe served as a good workbench and seat for a man named Young Doctor carving a totem pole.

A couple works at cutting and processing fish, perhaps halibut.

Makah families valued their children. Children got their names at a small feast following birth, but they could be given additional names later in life when their fathers held potlatches. Northwest Coast Indians believed that babies were reincarnations of people who had died in the past.

Makah children were taught to rely on the wisdom of their elders to make life easier for them. Even today, the elders are responsible for passing on the collective wisdom that the Makah people have acquired through thousands of years on the earth. The teachings are done through ceremonies and practical experience.

Makah women raised the children, made clothing, wove baskets, raised the furbearing dogs, gathered shellfish, berries, shoots, and roots, and preserved and prepared food. Woven baskets and wooden boxes were soaked to prevent the vessels

*Great fun in the surf in small canoes was also excellent training
for boys who would later take on adult responsibilities.*

from burning, since cooking was done over an open fire. In
another method of cooking, women put water into a cedar box
and then added glowing hot rocks to provide necessary heat.

Children helped their parents with household chores. From
their elders—their parents, grandparents, and older tribal
members—they learned the skills and techniques they would
need as adults. Children often used games or sports to improve
their skills. Boys had to undergo difficult training to make them
strong and brave. They swam in ice-cold water in the winter
time and played games that improved their athletic ability.
These included footraces and archery. In one such game, a
hoop made of cedar bark was rolled across a field or along the
beach. Boys tried to shoot arrows through it as it rolled. Girls
learned at an early age about housekeeping duties and gather-
ing and processing food.

A favorite game of both boys and girls—and adults, too—was called **shinny**. It was played on a field about 200 yards (180 m) long with goals on either end, as in football or soccer. Players had two sticks about 3 feet (1 m) in length. One was wide for hitting the ball, which was made of either wood or whalebone. The other stick was slender and hooked at the end, similar to a lacrosse stick, for carrying the ball. The object of the game was to get the ball across the opposing team's goal.

Shinny is a form of lacrosse, a game that was typical of Indian groups across the United States. There was no set number of players on a team. Sometimes there were a hundred or more players on each side. It could be rough. Often large bets were waged on the outcome. Injuries were common because there were few rules. Besides being fun and providing a form of exercise, the game required skills useful in combat, so it was part of a warrior's training. Many tribes called the game "the little brother of war."

Above all, games are used to teach self-respect, cooperation, leadership, and the ability to observe. As Greg Arnold, a Makah elder, explains, the skills children learn through games help prepare them to provide for their families and their future well-being. "Through the cooperation required to play team games, children learn to work together to move large canoes, build houses, preserve food for the winter, and hunt whales."

Tribal Government

Within each village several headmen gathered together as a council to decide village matters. The wealthiest headman was the most powerful. Whenever a headman died, his privileges were passed on to his eldest son. If there were no sons in the family, the position was passed to the eldest daughter. She then held the position of privilege until it could be passed on to the next male in line when he became of age.

Much of the social order was structured around the whale hunt. Whale hunters, especially the harpoonists, were the most powerful in the village's social order. The main whale hunter and his entire family, to whom his whaling knowledge and privileges would be passed on, were very influential. A person's possessions of goods, personal songs, dances, and stories were indicators of social status. Slaves were at the bottom of the social ladder.

Business of the village often followed the social status of its members. One example was in the distribution of food. The most important families received the first choices of

In the shape of an orca fin, this carved piece of cedar is studded with sea otter teeth. It was likely used in ceremonies by a person of great status.

meat from the whales. Within a long house, distribution of food and wealth followed from the headman to his eldest son and on down to the youngest child.

The Makah were a warring society. Their neighbors, the Quileute and Klallam, were their fierce enemies. The Klallam lived nearby in Puget Sound. The Quileute lived near the Makah on the Pacific side of the Olympic Peninsula. Warfare was often in retaliation for an act against one of the tribe's members. Another aim was to capture slaves, because slave ownership showed wealth and improved social status. Warriors would sneak into a village to steal people for slaves. First, warriors killed men and old people. Then they captured the people old enough to work but too young to fight. These people were taken as slaves but were not mistreated or beaten. Slaves were treated well so that they could work more. The Makah's enemies would then retaliate and capture Makah for slaves. The fierce fighting and capturing of slaves continued until well into the 19th century. During this time, many traditional practices were ended as a result of white settlement in the region, loss of population through disease, and pressure from the federal government of the United States.

Contemporary Life

Today many of the 2,200 Makah tribal members still live in the area of Neah Bay. Other tribal members or tribal descendants, however, live throughout the United States. The Makah reservation includes Neah Bay and the Ozette reservation site, which is farther south (see map). The Makah reservation is approximately 44 square miles (114 sq km) of land, and its people live in modern houses and enjoy the same conveniences as any American family. Makah children attend a primary school and high school at Neah Bay, and many go on to college.

Many Makah still make a living fishing for salmon and other species. At Neah Bay a large marina docks more than 200 commercial fishing and leisure boats owned by both Makah and non-Makah people. The Makah also have their own salmon hatchery on the Sooes River. A large number of summer tourists come to participate in the area's great fishing.

The U.S. government now recognizes the Makah Tribal government, which has a Tribal Council to make decisions. The Tribal Council is made up of five members, and it determines

Makah students, like others all across the country, take a bus to school.

*A Makah woman shows young visitors
local crabs, part of the bounty of the sea.*

regulations for its own members. The council members are voted into office by tribal members in a general election held every two years. However, tribal government and tribal members must still abide by laws set by the U.S. government.

The Makah quit hunting whales in the 1920s. Commercial whaling was banned worldwide in 1986 due to the dwindling numbers of whales left in the ocean. Recently the Makah submitted a request to the U.S. government and the International Whaling Commission (IWC) to regain their whaling rights promised forever in the 1855 Treaty of Neah Bay. In their request, the Makah asked permission to kill up to five whales per year. The IWC granted the Makah the right to hunt up to five gray whales annually.

That decision and the plans of the Makah to actively hunt whales led to controversy. Some people strongly believe that whales should not be killed by anyone for any reason. The Makah say that whaling is so important to keeping their culture strong that they must hunt whales as their ancestors did. In the fall of 1998 some

*Commercial fishing and leisure boats
dock at the Makah Marina at Neah
Bay, along with traditional Makah
boats such as* Hummingbird Canoe.

Contemporary Life ◆ 37

groups said that they would interfere with the Makah hunt and force them to stop. However, in that year the gray whales did not come close enough to shore for the Makah to find and hunt them.

The next year, on May 17, 1999, Makah hunters did catch a gray whale. The event marked the resumption of a tribal ritual that goes back for thousands of years. For over 70 years, the Makah have not hunted gray whales because commercial hunters had almost driven the world's whales to extinction. Now, thanks to preservation efforts, the gray whales are no longer endangered, and the United States government feels hunting a few of them each year will not cause any harm. For the Makah people, the renewal of this important cultural tradition is considered essential to the tribe's well being. Whale meat and blubber was once a central part of the Makah diet and culture.

The Makah hope the whale hunt will bring a spiritual revival

Makah people, including young children, wade into the water to touch the hunted whale, a Makah tradition, in May 1999.

to the tribe. So many years had passed since the last hunt that many of the ceremonies and prayers associated with whale hunting were in danger of being lost forever. Fortunately, some Makah elders still know the correct prayers and how to prepare the whale meat and render its oil. As one of the hunters said after the whale had been brought ashore to the cheers and chants of the Makah people who witnessed the event, "It's a proud day for our nation. I pray to our creator. I've waited a long time for this day. Prayed. Prayed. Prayed."

During "Makah Days," a summer celebration open to everyone, people enjoy planked salmon, prepared in the traditional way.

Makah people are still taught traditional ways. They are taught to respect the Earth and all its animals. Some are taught the traditional ceremonies so they may be passed down to their children and their children's children. Some are taught traditional crafts, such as weaving and wood carving. But Makah people also have jobs in businesses and the community like any other American people. Strictly following the traditional ways would be impractical today. The Makah have adapted enough to coexist with the non-Indians while still maintaining their strong heritage and sense of honor.

Girls perform a harpoon dance during the annual "Makah Days" celebration.

Makah Game

The Makah often played a game called Soktis. Many tribes in the Northwest as well as the Central Plains have a variation of this game.

Soktis is played with two hollow bones, each about 2 inches (5 cm) long. Each bone is decorated with circles with a red dot in the middle of each circle. One of the bones has black thread wrapped around the middle. Two teams face each other and take turns hiding the bones in their hands and guessing who has the "good" bone—the one with the red circles and no black thread.

Make your own version of the Soktis game by first finding two sticks to hide. They should be exactly the same in appearance and measure about 2 inches (5 cm) long. Use a marker or a piece of tape to make a black mark around the center of one of the sticks. Next you will need twenty objects to represent the score. Maybe you could use twenty pennies.

Earlier this century, men played the game of Soktis for pennies. The man with arms folded is hiding the small bones that make the pieces.

The stick with the black marker is the "bad" stick. The object of the game is to guess which hand has the "good" stick, or the stick without the mark.

Start by dividing your friends into two teams and sit across from each other. Place the twenty pennies in the middle of the floor. The first team picks one person to hide the sticks. That person decides which hand to hide the bad stick in. When he has carefully concealed the sticks in his fists, he holds his closed hands up. Then the opposing team picks one person to guess. He or she guesses which hand has the good stick. The hider then opens his hands. If the guesser has guessed the hand with the good stick, he earns one of the pennies from the middle for his team. He can then guess again with a new hider. If the guesser has guessed the hand with the bad stick, he loses a turn for his team. Then the second team gets to take the sticks and choose someone to hide them. The game goes on until all the pennies are earned from the middle.

The team with the most pennies wins!

Makah Prayer

This is a prayer that is used by the Makah.

Father in heaven, look down at us,
have pity on us, take our hands and put us
on the straight road, look after our souls
so that we may be able to serve you
with deepest reverence and in truth, for we need you
every day of our lives to walk straight always.

Source: *Makah Cultural and Research Center.*

Makah Recipe

Buckskin Bread

Adult supervision is required.

4 cups flour
2 heaping teaspoons baking powder
1 teaspoon salt
2 heaping tablespoons shortening
$1\frac{1}{2}$ cups water

Sift flour, baking powder, and salt into bowl. Add shortening. Mix it up well. Add water and mix with your hands until dough is soft. Knead dough on floured cookie sheet. Press dough into one large long, flat loaf. Bake at 450° for 20 minutes. Serve hot or cold with butter and jam or honey.

Makah Chronology

1492	Christopher Columbus, Italian explorer sailing for Spain, makes first contact with Indians of the Americas.
1559–1605	Spanish forces explore the west coast of North America.
1774	Contact with Juan Pérez Hernandez, Spanish explorer
1778	Contact with James Cook, English explorer
1784	Cook's journals published; fur trading increases.
1820	Most small, furbearing sea mammals on Northwest Pacific Coast disappear due to overharvesting for fur trade.
1855	Treaty of Neah Bay with U.S. government establishes Makah reservation and secures Makah whaling rights.
1861	James G. Swan conducts the first census of the Makah Reservation and counts 654 people.
1862	Trading ship brings smallpox from San Francisco.
1863	The first Indian Agent, Henry Webster, is assigned to Neah Bay.
1866	Makah people are hired by whites to work on commercial sealing boats.
1885	The first schooner is purchased by a Makah.
1890s	Makah schooner owners begin to employ whites.
1897	The U.S. government bans seal hunting.
1920s	Makah whale hunting ceases due to the scarcity of the animals.
1924	The Makah people and all other American Indians become U.S. citizens.
1930s	Salmon fishing replaces halibut fishing.
1931	First paved road built to connect Neah Bay with the "outside world" at Port Angeles, Washington.

1936	The Makah tribe ratifies its Tribal Constitution.
1970	Discovery of Ozette site
1979	The Makah Cultural and Research Center opens.
1997	Decision by International Whaling Commission permits Makah to resume whale hunting.
1998	Whales on their winter migration fail to appear near Neah Bay.
1999	First successful official whale hunt in 70 years conducted in May.

Glossary

Assimilation The U.S. government's attempt to force Indians to abandon their culture and integrate into mainstream American society.

Bow The front part of a boat or ship.

Headman The head of a long house household.

Kelp A type of very long seaweed that grows thickly in "forests" along the Pacific Coast of North America. It is a favorite habitat for sea otters to live and play in.

Kwih-ditch-chuh-ahtx The Makah name for themselves, which in English means "People who live by the rocks and seagulls."

Long houses Large, permanent dwellings made out of cedar.

Makah The name given to the Makah by their neighboring tribes, which means "generous with food."

Potlatch Derived from the Chinook word for "giving," a ceremony performed to show honor and earn status. Many gifts are given to honored guests.

Reservation A usually small area of land the government reserved for the Indians to live on.

Shinny A popular Makah game similar to lacrosse.

Smallpox A very contagious disease, often deadly, caused by a virus. A person with smallpox has a high fever and puss-filled bumps on the skin that can leave deep, permanent scars.

Tuberculosis A highly contagious disease of the lungs.

Further Reading

Cohlene, Terri. *Clamshell Boy: A Makah Legend.* Watermill Press, 1990.

Hoyt-Goldsmith, Diane. *Totem Pole.* Lawrence Migdale, 1990.

Lyons, Grant. *Pacific Coast Indians of North America.* Julian Messner, 1983.

National Museum of the American Indian. *Stories of the People: Native American Voices.* Smithsonian Institution and Universe Publishing, 1997.

Stewart, Hilary. *Stone, Bone, Antler & Shell: Artifacts of the Northwest Coast.* University of Washington Press, 1996.

Viola, Herman J. *North American Indians: An Introduction to the Lives of America's Native Peoples, From the Inuit of the Arctic to the Zuni of the Southwest.* Crown Publishers, 1996.

Sources

Bock, Paula. "A Whaling People: The Makah Hunt for Tradition and Memories of Whaling." *The Seattle Times Magazine*. (November 26, 1995.)

Cohlene, Terri. *Clamshell Boy: A Makah Legend*. Watermill Press, 1990.

Collins, Cary C. "Subsistence and Survival; The Makah Indian Reservation, 1855-1933." *Pacific Northwest Quarterly*, Vol. 87, No. 4, (Fall 1996): 180–193.

Colson, Elizabeth. *The Makah Indians, A Study of an Indian Tribe in Modern American Society*. The Manchester University Press and The University of Minnesota Press, 1953.

Indians of the Northwest, Traditions, History, Legends, and Life. Petra Press, Michael Friedman Publishing Group, Inc., 1997.

Kirk, Ruth. *Hunters of the Whale, An Adventure in Northwest Coast Archaeology*. William Morrow and Company, 1974.

National Museum of the American Indian. *Stories of the People: Native American Voices*. Smithsonian Institution and Universe Publishing, 1997.

Internet Source: The Makah Nation on Washington's Olympic Peninsula.

More information can be found on the World Wide Web site at http://www.makah.com

Visitors are welcome to see the Makah Cultural and Research Center, P.O. Box 169, Neah Bay, Washington 98357, phone: (360) 645-2771.

Index

Numbers in italics indicate illustration or map.